CLASSROOM TEACHING IDEAS

DR DHEERAJ MEHROTRA

Contents

Preface

"Classroom Teaching Ideas" is a requisite for making a difference in the Teaching-Learning Attributes towards Success.

The book features Managing Distractions Within Classrooms and favours the learning as a part of the Kaizen approach toward continuous development. The concept deals significantly towards making a difference towards literacy as a science and an art and which can be excelled using the power of intelligence with practice.

A priority on cards for educators! Best & Cheers!

Dheeraj Mehrotra

www.authordheerajmehrotra.com

tqmhead@aol.com

CHAPTER ONE

TEACHING IDEAS

Dear Teachers welcome to the Classroom Teaching Ideas, with a notion to make learning a priority for all.

Let us all learn about the Importance of Teaching Excellence:

Identifying the Classroom Distractions is a priority for the New Age Learning. As Educators, we need to explore the contest of learning with an exception.

The concern comes to our minds, why use a teaching strategy?

It is more like an Instructional Method that a teacher adopts to meet a learning objective.

It also aids a teacher in creating the right learning environment.

Well, for sure, the teaching methods foster and improve students learning journey. They are essential for students to make learning more conceptual and contextual.

A teaching strategy for a student's friendly classroom need not necessarily be very fancy; it can be engaging, straightforward, and less time-consuming.

To plan the teaching strategies, teachers need to consider the effectiveness and active participation of the students.

As an educator, it is necessary to prepare and set transparent and fair expectations that have a positive attitude, be mindful, and use a teaching strategy that is inquiry-driven, creative, and innovative.

Assure any of your teaching strategies should not be boring. We need to consider the lack of focus among the kids as a priority.

Some of the Teaching Strategies feature as follows:

1. Lecturing

Lecturing can mean an instructional talk, or it can take the form of a stern, one-sided conversation. It is in part through engaging students in interaction, using questions and answers, that some of the limitations of lectures can be overcome. The course has to be Lively, Educative, Creative, Thought-provoking, Understanding, Relevant and Enjoyable.

2. Circle Time Activities

A Circle time, also called group time, refers to a group of people sitting together for an activity involving everyone. Circle time is usually light and fun and aims to get children ready for learning. Consider the three basic questions of Why, What, and How.

3. Simulation Method

Activating classrooms via Simulations refers to instructional scenarios where the learner is placed in a "world" defined by the teacher. They represent a reality within which students interact. The teacher controls the parameters of this "Engagement" and uses it to achieve the desired instructional results.

4. Modelling Method

Modelling during teaching is an instructional strategy in which the teacher demonstrates a new concept or approach to learning, and students learn by observing. Whenever a teacher explains a concept forto a student, that teacher is modelling. It activates engagement in an absolute sense.

5. Online Learning Tools

These are the Most Popular Digital Education Tools For Teachers And Learners. The most common ones include Edmodo, an educational tool that connects teachers and students and assimilates into a social network. Google Classrooms and Kahoot are other commonly used platforms.

6. Game Simulation

As one of the innovative ways of teaching, the use of simulation games implies that the teacher values the unique needs of individual students. Learning is an active process rather than a passive one during this process. It encapsulates the importance of students‘ examining their values and the values of others in particular.

7. Collaborative Problem Solving

Very collaborative problem-solving acts as "the capacity of an individual to effectively engage in a process whereby two or more agents attempt to solve a problem by sharing the understanding and effort required to come to a solution and pooling their knowledge and skills in totality. It activates learning by doing hands-on.

8. Discussion Groups

The Discussion method of teaching is a group activity which involves the teacher and the student in defining the problem and deriving its solution. It is a constructive process that involves listening, thinking, and deriving conversation skills on priority.

9. Peer Instruction

Peer teaching involves one or more students teaching other students in a particular subject area and builds on the belief that "to teach is to learn twice" (Whitman, 1998)." For students, peer learning can lead to improved attitudes and a more personalised, engaging, and collaborative learning experience, leading to higher achievement. The experience can deepen their understanding of the subject and impart confidence to peer teachers.

10. Active Learning

Active learning is an approach to instruction that involves actively engaging students with the course material through discussions, problem-solving, case studies, role plays and other methods. The process is towards giving students a time limit to complete the task. The strategy identifies to Stop the activity and debrief. Call on a few students or groups of students to share their thoughts and tie them into the next steps of your lecture.

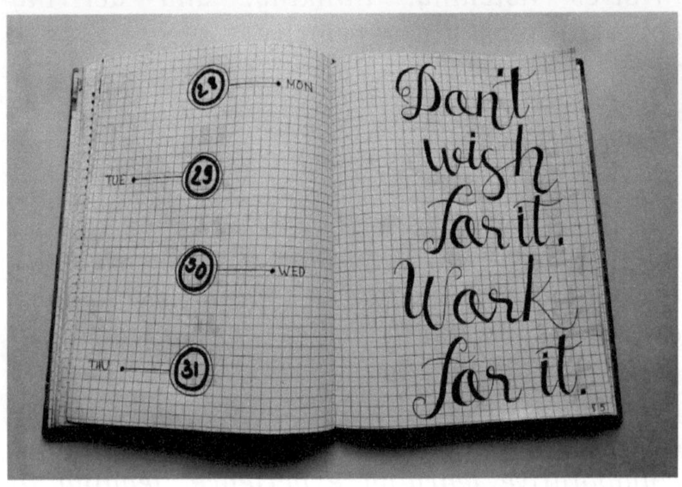

11. Project-Based Learning

Project-Based Learning is a teaching method in which students gain knowledge and skills by working for an extended period to investigate and respond to an authentic, engaging, and complex question, problem, or challenge. Project-based teachers ensure that students understand the learning goals and why they matter towards catching them young and innocent.

12. Unit Tests

Unit tests are conducted in the school to evaluate the summative assessment of the teaching-learning process. The main aim of the unit test is to isolate each unit of the system to identify, analyse and fix the defects. The test is different from assessment and evaluation in the following manner towards excellence.

13. Assignments

The Assignment method is the most common teaching method in schools, particularly in the teaching of Science. It is a technique usually used in the teaching and learning process. It is an instructional technique that comprises guided information, self-learning, writing skills and report preparation. It also includes simple homework assignments as one of the standard learning and evaluation methods.

14. Classroom Quizzing and Brain Gym:

Ask questions and make their brain work brighter. Example: Ask them to make the number 9 using their thumb altogether. Ask them to write their first name in ENGLISH using their index finger in the air.

15. Remedial Teaching

Identify weak students and engage them through peer learning. Involve them through partners such as 12.00 O Clock Partner or other time frames. This can even happen before assembly or after school.

16. Presentations

Engage them through the presentation skills via Technology. Some widely used presentation platforms include PREZI, MS Powerpoint and KEYNOTE.

17. Zoom In

Let the students observe gradual portions of an image and ask them to write and engage in writing. Ask them what new things they see. How does it change their thinking? Repeat the reveal and questioning until the whole image is revealed.

18. Chalk Talk

Using the Chalk Talk Strategy to engage them via homework analysis. The chalk talk method is an excellent way to ignite shy students. It engages the learners, promotes independent thinking and allows them to have an equal say. Here the teacher tells the students to analyse their thought analysis. The students rotate as a team via different prompts. The output is shared in public.

19. Work Books & Step Inside Routine

It gives the option to students to answer questions using Step Inside virtually. You let them step inside the character of the individuals. It is like stepping inside the situation in particular. Suitable for English, History, and exploring historical events from a specific perspective. Example Thinking or wondering about a soldier's perspective.

20. Posters and Reading Conference

Showcase the Posters and ask the children to read and interact. This goes via interactions randomly with peers and the teachers. It integrates Visual Literacy like I see I wonder. The use of posters and the opportunity to read the content individually or as per the lucky system works wonders.

21. Self-Learning Tools

This is a live example of using learning tools as a practical approach. Some online tools include Google Digital Garage, LinkedIn Learning, Coursera, Khan Academy, edX and Academic

Earth.

22. Competitions

This includes the various formats like Debates/ Interactions/ Recitation/ Writing/ Fashion Shows/ Speech Contest/ Case Study Presentations.

23. Object-Based Learning

Object-based learning is a form of active learning. A student-centred learning approach is an educational method that actively actively actively us classroom learning via engagement as a priority. To make it effective, the students must first practice the imparted skills of identifying and describing the main topic or activity in a class and giving some coherent, sequenced details. The idea is to catch them young and innocent towards learning as the ultimate.

25. Club Activities

This leads to bodily awareness, independent thinking, problem-solving and reasoning, positive self-image, talent management and collaboration & teamwork. The other activities include co-curricular activities such as public speaking, debate and dramatics, creative writing, eco-club, quizzing, astronomy, dance, photography, philately, trekking, film appreciation and even cooking.

26. Adaptive Teaching

Adaptive teaching as an educational method aims to achieve a common instructional goal with learners whose individual differences, such as prior achievement, aptitude, or learning styles, differ. It assists in providing personalised learning, aiming at providing efficient, effective, and customised learning paths to the learners. It also helps the teachers to engage each student. It is a student data-driven approach to adjusting the direction and pace of learning, enabling the delivery of personalised learning at scale in totality.

27. Cross Over Learning

The concept of crossover learning refers to a comprehensive understanding of learning that bridges formal and informal learning settings toward teaching excellence. It is one of the techniques used to provide personalised learning and aims to provide efficient, effective, and customised learning paths to engage each student.

28. Case Study

The case study methodology incorporates learning by engaging the students in discussing specific scenarios that represent real-world examples, such as Distractions Within Classrooms. This method is learner-centred, with intense interaction between participants, such as brainstorming. This further makes them develop skills, build their knowledge and work together as a group to examine the case.

29. Self-Learning

Using Google Earth Educational Tools. This helps visualise the abstract concepts across a global canvas, allowing students to connect what they learn inside to what they experience in their daily lives, community, and the larger world. Google Earth's creation tools allow will enable you to create your projects.

30. Team Projects

This may include creating a poster, making a PowerPoint presentation, designing a model, making a shoebox diorama, Using a 3-panel display board, Making a timeline, creating a board game incorporating key elements, and writing a poem.

31. Research Projects

Research-based teaching means that students conduct research independently and with an open outcome in their courses. This teaching and learning methodology focuses on the joint acquisition of new skills by lecturers and students. This requires the teachers to reflect on their role as teachers and learners.

32. Gesturing

This form of teaching integrates the learner's gestures, allowing indexing of conceptual instability moments. The teachers, during this process, make use of those gestures to gain access to a student's thinking. The learners discover novel ideas from the gestures produced during a lesson during the process.

33. Instructional Videos

This is a prevalent methodology to integrate the showcase of learning using videos. The instructions electronically in videos guide the students to follow a specific path, and learning is depicted during the process.

34. Social Media

The ultimate use of social media in teaching assists the students with the ability to get more helpful information. It makes them connected with learning groups and other educational platforms online. It allows the students to share their queries, concerns, and comments, making education convenient. These tools allow the students and institutions to explore multiple opportunities to improve learning methods.

35. Humour

Humour in the classroom explores the inception of Teaching styles that have changed significantly over the years. It allows the switch from the traditional way education was delivered through recitation and memorisation techniques. In contrast, the modern way of doing things involves interactive methods with humour as a priority now for sure with the march of time and tide as a reality in practice for schools and teachers need to dwell as a hobby for now. The inception is eyed and segmented towards the participative nature of students within classrooms to connect and make learning a priority for both the teacher and the learner in momentum to share the cause of education, making the best for all.

36. Panel Discussion

During this teaching process, the process is initiated through observation and listening. In a Panel Discussion, a designated or an invited group of students act as a panel, and the remaining class members act as the audience. The committee further discusses the selected questions and topics in particular. A panel leader is chosen, and they summarise the panel discussion and opens the conversation to the audience. A question and answer session follows the process for clarity and collaboration.

37. Modelling

Modelling is an instructional strategy in which the teacher demonstrates a new concept or an approach to make learning a priority with the preface of teaching excellence and WOW spectrum towards the taste and requirements of the learners. The students during this phase enjoy the learning through observation. The teaching is done by observing. Whenever a teacher demonstrates a concept for a student, that teacher is modelling as a measure.

38. Discovery Method

The Discovery Learning Method is mandated through the "Guided Discovery" format, which refers to a teaching and learning environment where students actively discover knowledge by exploring options through working and exploring ideas. It is a constructivist theory based on the idea that students construct their understanding and knowledge of the world by experiencing things and reflecting on those experiences. It is assisted through inquiry-based instruction and is considered a constructivist-based education approach.

39. Demonstration Method

As the word says, demonstration, the module covers showcasing with explanation in particular. It is used to communicate an idea with the assistance of visuals like flip charts, posters, PowerPoint, and other online or offline tools. A demonstration is a process of teaching someone how to make or do something step-by-step. It is suitable for science subjects.

40. Role Playing Method

Role-play is a technique that allows students to explore realistic situations by interacting with other people in an organised manner towards developing real-life skills and experiencing an environment of choice and chance. It provides an additional learning delight for the students, and they can very well understand the scenario being discussed during the process.

41. Oral Questions

This methodology allows the teacher to engage the students via assignments orally. It initiates and involves the teacher, where probing is conducted among the students. Here the questions are floated to think about what they know regarding a topic, and in the verbal format, they respond. The Questions typically allow the teacher to keep a point of the discussion focused on the intended objective and the learning objective through the involvement of all the students at length.

42. Questioning Method

This is an add on method to the Oral Questions and may include the written assignments. The objective is to engage the students via connections and jobs.

43. Discussion Method

Here we follow the collaborative exchange of ideas among the students to ignite students thinking, learning, problem-solving, understanding, and decision-making abilities.

44. Problem Based Learning

This identifies the engagement of the kids through Question or Assignment based learning. The teacher takes the problem/ assignment and works on it with the students and significant contributors. This acts as one of the easy-going tools to examine them during revision modules.

45. Assignments

This includes work assignments, routine jobs, class tests, homework and online reflections.

46. Make free and open source technologies available to teachers and students

The objective is towards specific connections via the directions from the UNESCO, Open educational resources and open access digital tools must be supported. Education cannot thrive with ready-made content built outside of the pedagogical space and outside of human relationships between teachers and students. Nor can education be dependent on digital platforms controlled by private companies.

47. Cross Over Learning

The crossover learning format entirely refers to a comprehensive understanding of learning that bridges a classroom's formal and informal learning settings. Experiences from everyday life can enrich the learning through this medium; informal learning can be deepened by adding questions and knowledge from the school. This format aims to combine the strengths of formal and informal learning environments and seeks to provide students with the best of both. As per boardteachers.com, an effective method for crossover learning involves teachers proposing a question or problem in the classroom to be solved during museum visits or field trips. Children can learn by collecting photos, taking down notes, or asking other people for their thoughts. They then present what they learned back in the classroom to illuminate the given problem further.

48. Dramatic Method

It is more like drama in teaching or dramatics in education. This, at random, allows students to explore the curriculum using several of Gardner's multiple intelligences. Here the kids are fully involved in learning with drama as a practice. They are immersed in the subject through the activities and do role plays of characters on the subject of learning. The process activates at length the development of their skills and, particularly, their bodies, minds, and emotions, yielding creativity and innovation as a common practice.

49. Pen Pals

A coined word of yesteryears has an interpreted meaning today. Teachers and educators worldwide share their experience with global project-based learning through PenPal platforms. One of the schools practising this says: We set the children up with their email addresses and put these under one central email alias. This allowed the teachers to screen each email exchange to ensure it was appropriate and then prepare spelling lists and topic word banks based on the sales. We moved to weekly discussions because the messages were now arriving within seconds of hitting "send," and we moved to weekly deals. This allowed our students to breeze through the usual "getting to know you" questions and move on to topics that allowed for meaningful cultural interactions.

50. Audio Tutorial Lessons

Also known as PODCASTING in a novel sense, the format is widely used in schools. The audio tutorial instruction is the most complete and well-documented auditory presentation method among teachers.

51. Mobile Applications

Mobile apps help in systematic learning in a big way. The best part is that Mobile learning (m- learning) is education via the Internet with the help of personal mobile devices. This is encompassed with BYOD- Bring Your Device format in schools where devices like tablets and smartphones assist learning to a better level. It helps obtain learning materials through mobile apps, social interactions and online educational hubs.

52. Flowcharts

This is a diagrammatic way of teaching where each activity is represented through a symbol. These are joined through the direction arrows and are connected through lines.

53. Brain Storming

This is an act of idea generation. This activity encourages students to focus on a topic and contribute to the free flow of ideas. Ideally, it is initiated by the teacher as a facilitator who may begin a brainstorming session by posing a question or a problem or by introducing a topic. In-process, the students express possible answers, relevant words, and ideas.

54. Simulation Games

The use of simulation games within classrooms implies that the teacher values the unique needs of individual students. It signifies that learning is an active process and hence has to equip with innovation and creativity.

55. Psychomotor Development Methods

Psychomotor learning is demonstrated by physical skills such as movement, coordination, and manipulation of learning traits among students. It delivers organised patterns of muscular activities guided by signals from the environment.

56. Inquiry Method

Inquiry-based learning is an approach that encapsulates the student's role in the learning process. Rather than the teacher telling students what they need to know, students are encouraged to explore the material, ask questions, and share ideas.

57. Ensure scientific literacy within the curriculum.

As guided and reflected by UNESCO, this is the right time for deep reflection on curriculum, particularly as we struggle against the denial of scientific knowledge and actively fight misinformation. Teachers can help and guide students using various topics via scientific literacy.

58. Webinars

A webinar is an interface over the Internet. A much talked about and explored during the CORONA times globally. The webinar allows interaction between the students and the professors online. When used in a classroom as a medium of teaching, it helps remove the scepticism from the minds of the shy students to raise their hands and ask questions in a classroom full of students—a very effective tool in particular.

59. Process Approach Method

The process approach is a method of thinking applied to understand and plan the sequence and interactions of processes in the system. Teaching here is integrated through a process and the interactions of these processes as part of the teaching and learning system in a classroom scenario.

60. Hands-on hands-On

Hands-on learning is a teaching pattern of imparting education in which children learn by doing themselves. Instead of simply listening to a teacher on the specified subject, the student engages with the subject matter to solve a problem or create something via hands-on experience via engagement and teamwork.

61. Seminars

A seminar is an opportunity to learn or explore learning via interactions. Particularly in academics, a meeting may have several purposes, such as a lecture, where the participants engage in the discussion of an academic subject to gain a better insight into the subject matter. For a typical classroom scenario, it works as an option for learning with pleasure.

62. Chalk and Talk

A Chalk Talk is a much preferred and silent activity that allows all students to reflect on what they know and then share their thinking and wonderings while connecting to their classmates' thoughts. "Chalk & Talk" is a formal teaching method with a blackboard and the teacher's voice as its focal point. This method is used in classrooms across the world. Despite the name, there is no chalk involved with the advent of technology, only paper and pencils, markers or digital devices. Laboratory

The School labs are an excellent place for students, which help them enhance their learning by understanding the theoretical concepts of science taught in classrooms. The set-up of the student-friendly has to be encapsulated. Well-designed laboratories make science experiments fun and help students achieve good academic results. It salutes the framework of learning through demonstrations and hands-on learning.

64. Content Analysis

Content analysis is a research method that allows the qualitative data collected in research to be analysed systematically and reliably so that generalisations can be made about the categories of interest to the researcher. It is one of the ACTIVE RESEARCH activities by educators, and the research findings help deliver learning as a priority for schools.

65. Reciprocal Teaching

Reciprocal teaching is an instructional activity where students become the teacher in small group reading sessions. Common teaching refers to a classroom activity where students are shown strategies to understand a reading better. As one of the periodic models of education, RT helps students learn to guide group discussions using four techniques: summarising, question generating, clarifying, and predicting in particular.

66. Assignment Method

With the help of the Assignment Method, evaluation based learning is possible. Using this process of assignment method, the teacher delivers an assignment with clear instructions, milestones, objectives and grading criteria based on an outcome that students need to achieve as an activity scheduled over a phase of time. The teacher accordingly monitors and further delivers the feedback to students as they solve the assignment and share the input towards improvement.

67. Micro Teaching

It is a part of teacher training, but it helps students learn a lot. Microteaching can also define as a teaching technique mainly used in teachers‘ pre-service education to train them systematically by allowing them to experiment with main teabehavioursviors real-life life scenarios. It more o less helps as a revision module on the go, which enables teacher trainees to practice a skill by teaching a short lesson to a small number of pupils. Usually,y a micro class of 5 to 10 minutes is taught to four or five fellow students.

68. Mastery Learning

Mastery learning, also known as competency-based teaching, is a set of group-based, individualised teaching and learning strategies based on the preface that students will achieve a high level of understanding in a given domain if given enough time. It ensures that the students obtain mastery of a given topic before moving on to the next unit. The objective is to gain high achievement levels through active instruction, time, and perseverance.

69. Direct Instructions

Direct instruction is a teacher-directed teaching method. This means that the teacher stands in front of a classroom and presents the information. The teachers give explicit, guided instructions to the students. To make it practical and straightforward, direct instruction refers to instructional approaches that are structured, sequenced, and led by teachers, and the presentation of academic content to students by teachers, such as in a lecture or demonstration within the classrooms over a specified interval.

70. Personalised Instruction

It is one of the basic earning and teaching. It refers to instruction-based learning in which the pace of knowledge and the instructional approach are optimised for the needs of each learner. As a Learner Centric and Specific learning format, it fascinates learning towards priority. Learning objectives, instructional strategies, and content (and sequencing) may vary based on learner needs.

71. Recitation

In a general sense, a recitation is an act of reciting from memory or a formal reading of prose or other writing before an audience. The definition of a recitation is the telling of details, or the act of saying something that's bememorisedzed out loud, or the thing that is read.

72. Memorization

It defines the means of learning by self. Many students feel like they simply do not have strong memory skills. Fortunately, though, memorizingmemorisingst for an elite group of people born with the right skills—anyone can train and develop their memorising.

73. Reasoning

This concerns the critical way of learning and exploring the new unknown. Logical reasoning determines if algorithms will work by predicting what happens when the algorithm's steps - and the rules they consist of - are followed. Predictions from each algorithm can be used to compare solutions and decide on the best one.

74. Social-Emotional Learning

Social-emotional learning (SEL) develops self-awareness, self-control, and interpersonal skills that are important for school, work, and life success. People with strong social-emotional skills prove to be better in Italy's life challenges and benefit academically, professionally, and socially.

75. Instructional scaffolding

Instructional scaffolding is a process through which a teacher provides support to students to enhance learning and assist in the mastery of tasks. Here, the instructor systematically builds on students' experiences and knowledge while learning the new skills.

CHAPTER TWO

The Imaginative Educator

Not all classrooms of today are equipped with the parenting of new-age learning stream, which we observe from taste to tongue the new generation of age. A Teacher, who is now a ***FACILITATOR*** *in this generation, encapsulates a new order of delivery with the extension of a knowledge society and not a content delivery or an interpretation of book knowledge in real life. The innovation is the ultimate to generate interest in learning for the kids today. It mounts a lot of energy and thoughts to be an innovative educator who is of particular requisite to deliver the knowledge to today's cyber society.*

The mantra is Engage Me or Enrage Me, *from the side of the students at large.*

Indeed, the teachers are no longer the sole imparters of knowledge. Still, they need to empower the students to learn at a pace and leisure through personal learning networks to keep their unique talents and interests. The teachers don't end after the class is over but on the jolt for 24 hours around the cyber linkage or other social networks. There is no wall now or the boundary of learning. The innovative educator has to evolve a personal learning network for improvement first. It has to reach the students as well where there is no boundary or limitation in a big way. It is a way to build a classroom and network of learning. The change or the shift here is that we can connect and share ideas which are not so in the one to many modes of classroom learning.

The new age imaginative teacher has to be fertile in laminating the knowledge from roots and sharing the same with his students of all ages and figures. It also reflects a Quality Teacher to share the unknown and the unnoticed with the religious sentiments of repute.

The fact lies in the Teacher being an Innovator of traits and essence to explore the attention in the classroom. The priority of taking Education and technology to go together laminates with the questions in our minds, viz. Should we do more or less? What about virtual schools? Interactive whiteboards? Cell phones? Facebook and Twitter? Should we let kids be out there on the 'net? Should we post their pictures? These are legitimate conversations, and each person has to make these kinds of decisions based on their comfort levels and according to the individual child's needs. They must be given an opportunity only when required but as a habit to my knowledge and interest.

The innovative learning is not limited to a physical space but an open learning scenario with a preface to one's comfort in his reading home at home or a TV room at large. It is very much unlike the classroom learning with the same group all day, all the time. Here the community is different, and the learning is more spectacular further. Here the teacher concerned is the one who has to be engaged and involved in the conversations as a leader or a facilitator further.

A priority for the Educators, policymakers and the private sector is the need to strive together and make India a global superpower by 2020. The five year plans in India root to new phases at times, but the delivery is hard to explode in particular.

As per the demands and research, the challenge is to create an integrated education system that:

- *Provides access to quality education that is practical, relevant, customised and effective*
- *Can adopt innovative ways (tech-based) to provide faster expansion of opportunities of education to all*
- *Looks for bridging the gap between education and employability*
- *Promotes social equality/economic viability*

One policy is not going to help all. The need of the hour is to have specific guidelines for various levels and areas of education specific to multiple regions.

As an academician, I feel that "Everyone is a genius. But if you judge a fish by its ability to climb a tree, it will live its whole life believing that it is stupid." as do one of the inventors of past years.

Cheers and Happy Learning.....

About The Author

Dheeraj Mehrotra, MS, MPhil, PhD (Education Management) honoris causa., a white and a yellow belt in SIX SIGMA, a Certified NLP Business Diploma holder, is an Educational Innovator, Author, with expertise in Six Sigma In Education, Academic Audits, Neuro-Linguistic Programming (NLP), Total Quality Management In Education, an Experiential Educator, a CBSE Resource towards School Assessment (SQAA), CCE, JIT, Five S and KAIZEN. He has authored over 40 books on Computer Science for ICSE/ ISC/ CBSE Students and over 50 books of academic interest for the field of education excellence and Six Sigma. A former Principal at De Indian

Public School, New Delhi, (INDIA) with an ample teaching experience of over Two Decades, he is a certified Trainer for Quality Circles/ TQM in Education and QCI Standards for School Accreditation/ Six Sigma in Education. He has also been honoured with the President of India's National Teacher Award in the year 2006 and the Best Science Teacher State Award (By the Ministry of Science and Technology, State of UP), Innovation in Education for his inception of Six Sigma In Education by Education Watch, New Delhi and Education World- Best Teacher Award, BOLT Learner Teacher Award by Air India, 'Innovation in Education Award 2016' by Higher Education Forum (HEF), Gujarat Chapter, among others.

He has developed over 150 FREE EDUCATIONAL MOBILE Apps for the Google Play Store exclusively for Teachers, Students and Parents. This work has been recognised by the LIMCA BOOK OF RECORDS & INDIA BOOK OF RECORDS as the only Indian to draw that feast. As a premier UDEMY Instructor, he has developed over 450 UDEMY. Dr Mehrotra is presently working as a PRINCIPAL at Kunwar's Global School, Lucknow in India. He has conducted over 1000 workshops globally on "Excellence In Education" integrated with Total Quality Management and Six Sigma, Technology

Integration in Education (TIE), Developing towards being ROCKSTAR TEACHERS, including Cyberspace, Cyber Security, Classroom Management, School Leadership & Management, and Innovative teaching within classrooms via Mind Maps, NLP and Experiential Learning in Academics. He is an active TEDx speaker and can be viewed on the youtube TEDx channel. He can be visited at www.authordheerajmehrotra.com

Books By The Same Author

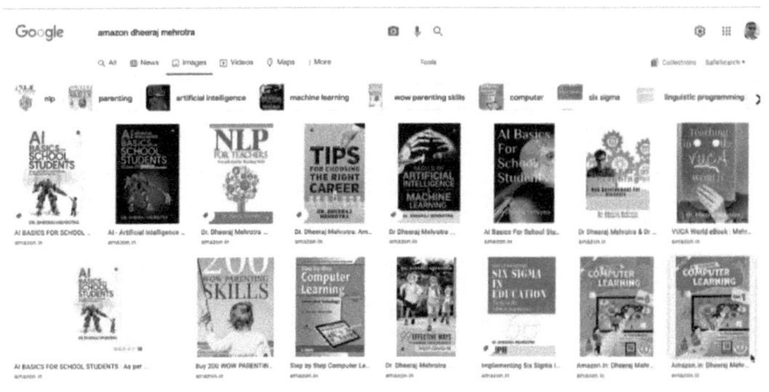

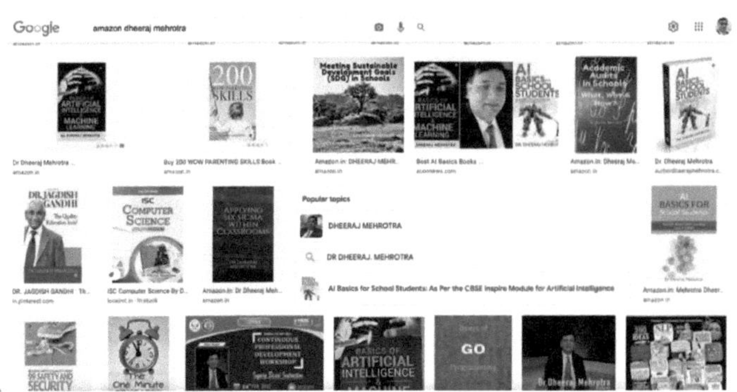

Visit: www.authordheerajmehrotra.com for more details.

9 798886 847208

Printed by Libri Plureos GmbH in Hamburg,
Germany